Called
Leader Guide

CALLED
HEARING AND RESPONDING TO GOD'S VOICE

Called

978-1-5018-7974-6

978-1-5018-7975-3 eBook

Called: DVD

978-1-5018-7978-4

Called: Leader Guide

978-1-5018-7976-0

978-1-5018-7977-7 eBook

Lessons from Six Biblical Characters

Called

Hearing and Responding to God's Voice

Susan Robb

Leader Guide
by Benjamin J. Dueholm

Abingdon Press / Nashville

CALLED:
HEARING AND RESPONDING TO GOD'S VOICE
LEADER GUIDE

978-1-5018-7976-0

19 20 21 22 23 24 25 26 27 28 — 10 9 8 7 6 5 4 3 2 1
MANUFACTURED IN THE UNITED STATES OF AMERICA

Contents

To the Leader

"Everyone who is a Christian is called," Susan Robb writes in the introduction of her book *Called: Hearing and Responding to God's Voice*. Christian life itself is a vocation—or calling—to following the teachings of Jesus, to discipleship, and to making new disciples in turn. But within that general calling, God gives us particular gifts, particular guidance, and particular opportunities to serve the world and the body of Christ in roles for which we are especially suited. When we try to discern whether we should marry or begin a family, whether to pursue one career or another, where and how to serve in church, and even how to speak and act as citizens and neighbors, we are discerning our callings.

This Leader Guide will prepare you to facilitate six sessions in a small group study of *Called*. Through the stories of six biblical figures—Abraham, Samuel, Esther, Jonah, Mary Magdalene, and the Beloved Disciple—who are called by God for certain tasks, this book explores what it means to listen for God's calling in our lives. Through the long delays, frustrating repetitions, moments of dread and doubt, and even outright resistance experienced by these figures, we will consider how to hear and answer God's particular calling for us. Far from being distant and otherworldly heroes of faith, these six characters all took indirect and sometimes difficult paths to the fulfillment of God's plans for them. People who have to navigate the modern world's diversity of voices and priorities on their way to answering God's vocation can take comfort, strength, and inspiration from their stories and their examples.

Chapter Summaries

CHAPTER ONE: FATHER ABRAHAM

In his 70s, Abram (not yet "Abraham") is called by God to leave his home to follow God to a new land that God promises to him and his descendants. Along the way he and his wife, Sarai (not yet "Sarah"), experience doubt and dismay, infertility and conflict, as well as some tragic mistakes by themselves and others. They also receive assurance from God, and new names to boot, before the child God promises them finally arrives. In the incremental nature of their journey and their continual call to place God at the center of their journey, we can see how God is present to us in our own fitful journeys.

CHAPTER TWO: HERE I AM!

Samuel is born as the answer to his mother's desperate prayer, and he is raised in the temple of God by the priest Eli in fulfillment of his mother's promise. Like most people, Samuel needed more than just his biological parents to raise him up and help him answer his call. As the priest, prophet of God, and judge of Israel, Samuel has to deliver hard words, keep the nation faithful, and find the people God was appointing to be their kings. His story reminds us that people of any age or stature or appearance can hear God's call.

CHAPTER THREE: A TIME SUCH AS THIS

Esther's story represents the power of a single person in a single moment to change the course of history. Set in Persia after the exile of many Jews from the land promised to Abraham, the Book of Esther concerns the titular heroine's rise to royal status and her daring work to thwart a plot by the king's advisor to destroy all the Jews in the kingdom. Ordinary people are called in these circumstances to take risks and make a difference. Even today, ordinary Christians are called to use the gifts and opportunities they have to work for justice and reconciliation.

CHAPTER FOUR: A MOST RELUCTANT PROPHET

When God calls Jonah to preach an oracle of destruction in the great enemy city of Nineveh, he does not merely doubt or hesitate, he flees God's voice as fast and as far as he can. But at sea and in the belly of the great fish that swallows him after he's cast overboard from the foundering ship, Jonah learns that God is already there, where Jonah seeks to flee. When Jonah does obey his calling and goes to Nineveh, the people hear his message and repent. Jonah's bitterness and God's message of mercy remind us that God can work through and despite our own reluctance.

CHAPTER FIVE: I HAVE SEEN THE LORD!

Mary Magdalene, one of the women who financially supported Jesus and his followers, becomes the first to proclaim the Easter event of the empty tomb and the first to speak with the risen Christ. Her generosity toward her community and her persistence in discipleship, to the point of coming to the tomb before anyone else, show us how to overcome our fears, our ingrained expectations, and even our reputation to share the good news.

CHAPTER SIX: LEANING IN

The disciples of Jesus are called out of their daily lives and responsibilities to follow Jesus and share his proclamation of the kingdom of God that has come near. Despite their doubts, they are commissioned to make disciples, to baptize, to teach, and to remember that Jesus is with them to the end of the age. The figure of the Beloved Disciple in John's Gospel becomes the image of our ideal relationship with Jesus and through him with God the Father—a relationship of intimacy and love that is reflected in our own service in the world.

Preparing to Lead This Study

- Pray for the guidance and insight of the Holy Spirit, for the participants in your group, and for your own growth as a disciple through the group process.
- Find, reserve, and prepare a suitable space for learning and conversation.
- Plan to begin and end on time. The sessions typically last 50 minutes to one hour.
- Supply Bibles for participants who don't bring their own. You may want to have multiple translations for comparison, or you may wish to simplify by providing multiple copies of the New Revised Standard Version.
- Obtain a markerboard or flip chart for discussion topics and responses. Include a "parking lot" for topics that need to be returned to later.
- Be sure to have a working DVD player and screen for viewing the video segments.
- Choose the activities that best fit your plan and allotted time for the group session.

- Plan to model the honesty and openness a small group study requires to be effective. Get comfortable answering the same questions you ask of the group.
- Prepare to be comfortable with the silence needed to encourage thoughtful answers. Plan to be deliberate about preventing a few voices from dominating conversation, and about encouraging people who need to think at more length before they speak.
- Be ready to respond patiently and without anxiety if strong feelings or difficult experiences are shared by participants.

Session Outline

This Leader Guide suggests that each session have discussion and/or activities centered on a corresponding video clip of author Susan Robb and chapter from her book *Called*. You may adjust the outline below to fit your group's needs.

- Session Goals
- Biblical Background
- Preparation
- Materials Needed
- Welcome and Icebreaker
- Prayer
- Video (DVD)
- Discussion
- Activity
- Closing

Vocation is a big topic, at once profoundly theological and close to home. It touches on all parts of our lives. May this study enrich your and your participants' ability and willingness to hear the many ways God calls us in our lives.

Father Abraham

Planning the Session

SESSION GOALS

Participants in the study should have the opportunity to

- describe the idea of "calling" as a matter of faith;
- talk about their own experiences of being "called" to different roles in their lives;
- hear and understand the story of Abraham and Sarah;
- connect the story of Abraham and Sarah to their own lives.

BIBLICAL BACKGROUND

If you can, it is helpful to read the whole story of Abraham in Genesis 12–25 before the group meets. Some of that material is touched on only slightly in the chapter, and some is not touched on at all, but having the whole story in mind can help with context of the specific events for yourself and your participants. It is also possible that some participants may be familiar with the story, have questions about it, and quite possibly find parts of it troubling. The most important passages for the discussion of the chapter are excerpted below.

Now the LORD said to Abram, "Go from your country and your kindred and your father's house to the land that I will show you. I will make of you a great nation, and I will bless you, and make your name great, so that you will be a blessing. I will bless those who bless you, and the one who curses you I will curse; and in you all the families of the earth shall be blessed."

So Abram went, as the LORD had told him; and Lot went with him. Abram was seventy-five years old when he departed from Haran.

Genesis 12:1-4

After these things the word of the LORD came to Abram in a vision, "Do not be afraid, Abram, I am your shield; your reward shall be very great." But Abram said, "O LORD God, what will you give me, for I continue childless, and the heir of my house is Eliezer of Damascus?" And Abram said, "You have given me no offspring, and so a slave born in my house is to be my heir." But the word of the LORD came to him, "This man shall not be your heir; no one but your very own issue shall be your heir." He brought him outside and said, "Look toward heaven and count the stars, if you are able to count them." Then he said to him, "So shall your descendants be." And he believed the LORD; and the LORD reckoned it to him as righteousness.

Genesis 15:1-6

When Abram was ninety-nine years old, the LORD appeared to Abram, and said to him, "I am God Almighty; walk before me, and be blameless. And I will make my covenant between me and you, and will make you exceedingly numerous." Then Abram fell on his face; and God said to him, "As for me, this is my covenant with you: You shall be the ancestor of a multitude of nations. No longer shall your name be Abram, but your name shall be Abraham; for I have made you the ancestor of a multitude of nations...."

God said to Abraham, "As for Sarai your wife, you shall not call her Sarai, but Sarah shall be her name. I will bless her, and moreover I will give you a son by her. I will bless her, and she shall give rise to nations; kings of peoples shall come from her." Then Abraham fell on his face and laughed, and said to himself, "Can a child be born to a man who is a hundred years old? Can Sarah, who is ninety years old, bear a child?"

Genesis 17:1-5, 15-17

So Sarah laughed to herself, saying, "After I have grown old, and my husband is old, shall I have pleasure?" The LORD said to Abraham, "Why did Sarah laugh, and say, 'Shall I indeed bear a child, now that I am old?' Is anything too wonderful for the LORD? At the set time I will return to you, in due season, and Sarah shall have a son." But Sarah denied, saying, "I did not laugh"; for she was afraid. He said, "Oh yes, you did laugh."

Genesis 18:12-15

PREPARATION

- Pray for your group participants.
- Make sure every participant has a copy of *Called: Hearing and Responding to God's Voice*, by Susan Robb. Encourage them to read the introduction and chapter 1 before the session.
- Read for yourself chapter 1 of *Called*, ideally twice—once to get the whole picture, and a second time to note important or memorable passages and topics of discussion.
- Read the Scripture passages included here and, if possible, the rest of the Abraham story. Keep a quality interpretive resource on hand for your or the group's questions.
- Read this session plan and consider what questions and activities will be most useful or important for your particular group, keeping in mind the limits of time available. You may want to write key questions on the markerboard or flip chart ahead of time.

MATERIALS NEEDED

- Bibles
- markerboard or flip chart
- video (DVD)
- paper and pens for participants to make notes
- nametags (optional)

During the Session

WELCOME AND ICEBREAKER (5-10 MINUTES)

Welcome the participants and invite them to fill in their nametags if you are using nametags. Introduce yourself and explain briefly why you were interested in leading this study.

Go around the room, giving each participant an opportunity to introduce himself or herself, to share one calling they have in life, and to tell one goal they have for this study. (*Answers may include work, parenting, caregiving, or a dedicated volunteer role.*)

Read or summarize:

- This study is about what it means to be called by God to do certain things in life.
- Calling, or "vocation," is an idea that includes both the gifts and the desires inside of us and the confirmation that comes from outside of us.
- "Calling" includes our work, our family, and our roles in the body of Christ; it includes our own reflections and the leading of God's Spirit.
- This book is about ordinary people called by God to do often extraordinary things. As we ponder their stories, perhaps we can better hear God's voice in our own lives.

PRAYER

Open with this or another prayer:
Let us pray.

Lord God, you have called your servants to follow your leading to places we can't yet see and by paths we do not know. We pray that you would open our hearts and minds to your voice this day and every day ahead, that we would clearly hear, and faithfully follow, your calling to us. In Jesus' name we pray. Amen.

VIDEO (8-10 MINUTES)

Introduce the segment: In this video, Susan Robb will talk about Abraham and Sarah and their journey "by stages" to answer the challenging calling God gave them. Look for connections between the video and the book. We'll discuss both together.

DISCUSSION (10-15 MINUTES)

Say or summarize: Early in the chapter, the author tells a story about her husband's ancestors moving from Oklahoma to Texas with "seemingly blind faith." They experience struggles and setbacks. The author writes about her own ups and downs in answering her call to ordained ministry. Do you have any family stories of migration? Or have you ever made a big and scary move yourself? How did it work out? What did it mean to your family?

Invite a participant to read Genesis 12:1-4.

Say or summarize:

- Susan Robb's former professor calls these four verses from Genesis the linchpin of the entire Bible.
- The verses begin God's relationship of covenant or promise with the descendants of Abraham and Isaac.
- This story comes to include the whole people of Israel, including Jesus, and, through Jesus, the whole Christian church.
- God calls Abraham to leave his home and go to a new land.
- God promises to bless Abraham and make him (and his descendants) a blessing to all the nations of the earth.
- Abraham takes the big step required to follow God's calling without questioning.

Ask the participants:

- What question(s) would you want to ask if you were in Abraham's situation?
- What did God promise to do for or give Abraham? (*offspring, land, blessing*)

Say or summarize: Even when we're answering God's calling, the author says, "We have doubts, reservations, and disappointments, and then something happens to remind us why we should continue pursuing the journey to which we have been called." God returns to Abraham to renew God's promise to him, giving him and Sarah the assurance they need to continue.

Ask the participants: Have you ever experienced assurance when you have struggled to answer a calling? (*Answers may include the challenge of caring for a new baby, the difficulty of adjusting to a new job or a new community, or the struggles of completing a degree or professional program.*)

BIBLE STUDY ACTIVITY (15–20 MINUTES)

This may be done in three groups or by the whole group, using one, two, or three of the options.

Divide the participants into three groups.

One group reads Genesis 16 (the story of Hagar and Ishmael) with an eye to answering these questions:

- What do Abram and Sarai do wrong? (*attempt to fulfill God's promise on their own, abandon Hagar and Ishmael*)
- Why do they do these things, and what were the consequences?
- Have you or someone close to you ever done something rash and destructive? If so, what were the consequences?
- Hagar leaves the story, but what does God do for or promise her? (*protection in the wilderness and a great name for her son*)
- Why do you think it was important for Abraham and Sarah's descendants to remember this story?

A second group reads Genesis 17 (the new names and the sign of the covenant) with an eye to answering these questions:

- How old is Abram in this passage? (*ninety-nine*)
- How does Abram respond to God renewing God's covenant with him? (*falls on his face, obeys command of circumcision*)
- Why does God change the names of Abram and Sarai, and what do their new names mean? (*Abraham = "Father of multitudes," Sarah = "Princess"*)
- A new name, or circumcision, can be thought of as "an outward and visible sign of an inward and spiritual grace." What else is like that, either in your faith or in your family life? (*Possibilities include worship, sacramental practices, vestments worn by ministers or clergy, changing a name at marriage, or family customs.*)
- Why do you think it was important for Abraham and Sarah's descendants to remember this story?

A third group reads Genesis 18:1-15 (the visit to Mamre and the laughter of Sarah) with an eye to answering these questions:

- Who visits Abraham and Sarah at the oaks of Mamre? (*God, either with two divine attendants or in a vision of the Trinity*)
- How do Abraham and Sarah react? (*offer extravagant hospitality*)
- What do the visitors say to Abraham, and how does Sarah react? (*renewed promise of a son; Sarah laughs*)
- What is your most memorable experience of giving or receiving hospitality?
- Why do you think it was important for Abraham and Sarah's descendants to remember this story?

After enough time has been allowed for the three groups to answer their questions, bring the group together and invite each group to share the story they read together and the questions they answered, paying special attention to the last question about the importance of the story.

Say or summarize:

- Abraham and Sarah experienced significant struggles, setbacks, and failures in answering their calling from God.
- But as the author says, "God is more faithful and patient with us than we are with God."
- Abraham and Sarah had to trust God's promises and guidance throughout their journey, rather than simply following a plan they fully knew.
- God proved to be faithful to them, and they became not only ancestors to a great multitude but a blessing to all.
- In our own lives we experience struggles, setbacks, and failures, but God still has plans for us.

CLOSING (10 MINUTES)

Say or summarize: The author writes:

Sometimes, even when we're answering God's call, the journey is difficult and doesn't seem clear, like traveling over a rocky passage in a covered wagon. We have doubts, reservations, and disappointments, and then something happens to remind us why we should continue pursuing the journey to which we have been called. While we can't see what lies ahead, we're reminded that God is faithful and can be trusted with our call.

And

Sometimes I work through doubts and frustrations by making lists of the blessings God has placed my life.

Abraham is blessed by God and becomes a blessing to the world. Take a few minutes of silence to make two lists on paper or in your head:

- a list of the ways in which God has blessed you in your life so far
- a list of the ways in which you are, or could be, a blessing to others

Invite the participants to

- share one or two items from each list;
- share whether these blessings, either given to them or intended for them to give, relate to a calling they have from God.

The author concludes the chapter:

> You are a beloved child of God, descendant of Abraham, set apart for great purposes. You are blessed to be a blessing to others; to show the world the depth of the love of God available to every person. May you listen for the voice of the One who wants to lead you "to the land that I will show you," trusting God will guide you, step by step, into a bright and unimaginable future.

And we will close with the prayer attributed by some to St. Teresa of Avila, recorded in the chapter:

May today there be peace within.
May you trust God that you are exactly where you are meant to be.
May you not forget the infinite possibilities born of faith.
May you use those gifts that you have received and pass on
*   the love that has been given to you.*
May you be content knowing you are a child of God.
Let this presence settle into your bones, and allow your soul
*   the freedom to sing, dance, praise and love.*
It is there for each and every one of us.

Amen.

Here I Am!

Planning the Session

SESSION GOALS

Participants in this session should have the opportunity to

- describe the people, apart from parents, who played a formative or parental role for them;
- identify the people who have given encouragement or confirmation in their callings;
- acknowledge and understand that a calling from God means having to say hard or uncomfortable things;
- look for the "interruptions" in their lives through which God speaks to them.

BIBLICAL BACKGROUND

Between the time of Abraham and Sarah and the time of Samuel, much has happened to the descendants of Abraham. Jacob, Abraham's grandson (also known as "Israel," or "he wrestles with God"), goes to Egypt with his sons and their families. After several centuries the children of Israel become numerous and are oppressed by the Egyptians. Through the leadership of Moses, God rescues them from slavery and leads them over decades through the wilderness. Eventually they settle in Canaan, where Abraham and Sarah are buried, and are governed by a series of judges. Samuel, who plays the role of priest and judge, also serves as God's prophet at the beginning of the age of Israelite kings. He anoints Saul and, later, David.

The account of Samuel's calling and the history of Israel during his lifetime is long and eventful, taking up most of the book of 1 Samuel. In fact he's so significant that the next book, concerning the rest of the royal career of David, is also named after him. If you have the time, it is well worth reading 1 Samuel 1–25. This session will focus on a few important episodes.

Samuel's story begins with his mother, Hannah, whose inability to have children causes her both disappointment and social stigma.

> She was deeply distressed and prayed to the LORD, and wept bitterly. She made this vow: "O LORD of hosts, if only you will look on the misery of your servant, and remember me, and not forget your servant, but will give to your servant a male child, then I will set him before you as a nazirite until the day of his death. He shall drink neither wine nor intoxicants, and no razor shall touch his head." . . .

> [Hannah] brought [Samuel] to the house of the LORD at Shiloh; and the child was young. Then they slaughtered the bull, and they brought the child to Eli. And she said, "Oh, my lord! As you live, my lord, I am the woman who was standing here in your presence, praying to the LORD. For this child I prayed; and the LORD has granted me the petition that I made to him. Therefore I have lent him to the LORD; as long as he lives, he is given to the LORD."

> She left him there for the LORD.

> 1 Samuel 1:10-11; 24b-28

> Hannah prayed and said,

>> "My heart exults in the LORD;
>>> my strength is exalted in my God.
>> My mouth derides my enemies,
>>> because I rejoice in my victory.

>> "There is no Holy One like the LORD,
>>> no one besides you;
>>> there is no Rock like our God.

> *Talk no more so very proudly,*
> > *let not arrogance come from your mouth;*
> *for the* LORD *is a God of knowledge,*
> > *and by him actions are weighed.*
> *The bows of the mighty are broken,*
> > *but the feeble gird on strength.*
> *Those who were full have hired themselves out for bread,*
> > *but those who were hungry are fat with spoil.*
> *The barren has borne seven,*
> > *but she who has many children is forlorn.*
> *The* LORD *kills and brings to life;*
> > *he brings down to Sheol and raises up.*
> *The* LORD *makes poor and makes rich;*
> > *he brings low, he also exalts.*
> *He raises up the poor from the dust;*
> > *he lifts the needy from the ash heap,*
> *to make them sit with princes*
> > *and inherit a seat of honor.*
> *For the pillars of the earth are the* LORD*'s,*
> > *and on them he has set the world.*
>
> *"He will guard the feet of his faithful ones,*
> > *but the wicked shall be cut off in darkness;*
> > *for not by might does one prevail.*
> *The* LORD*! His adversaries shall be shattered;*
> > *the Most High will thunder in heaven.*
> *The* LORD *will judge the ends of the earth;*
> > *he will give strength to his king,*
> > *and exalt the power of his anointed."*

1 Samuel 2:1-10

Compare this with the song of Mary, Mother of Jesus:

And Mary said,

> *"My soul magnifies the* LORD,
> > *and my spirit rejoices in God my Savior,*
> *for he has looked with favor on the lowliness of his servant.*
> > *Surely, from now on all generations will call me blessed;*
> *for the Mighty One has done great things for me,*
> > *and holy is his name.*

21

> *His mercy is for those who fear him*
> > *from generation to generation.*
> *He has shown strength with his arm;*
> > *he has scattered the proud in the thoughts of their hearts.*
> *He has brought down the powerful from their thrones,*
> > *and lifted up the lowly;*
> *he has filled the hungry with good things,*
> > *and sent the rich away empty.*
> *He has helped his servant Israel,*
> > *in remembrance of his mercy,*
> *according to the promise he made to our ancestors,*
> > *to Abraham and to his descendants forever."*
>
> Luke 1:46-55

As a boy, Samuel served God in the temple at Shiloh, alongside the priest Eli. This is where his prophetic calling begins:

> *The LORD called Samuel again, a third time. And he got up and went to Eli, and said, "Here I am, for you called me." Then Eli perceived that the LORD was calling the boy. Therefore Eli said to Samuel, "Go, lie down; and if he calls you, you shall say, 'Speak, LORD, for your servant is listening.'" So Samuel went and lay down in his place.*
>
> 1 Samuel 3:8-9

Samuel becomes the priest after God removes Eli's family for their transgressions. Samuel anoints Saul, the first king of Israel. Later, when God rejects Saul, Samuel goes to find David, the next king:

> *The LORD said to Samuel, "How long will you grieve over Saul? I have rejected him from being king over Israel. Fill your horn with oil and set out; I will send you to Jesse the Bethlehemite, for I have provided for myself a king among his sons." Samuel said, "How can I go? If Saul hears of it, he will kill me." And the LORD said, "Take a heifer with you, and say, 'I have come to sacrifice to the LORD.' Invite Jesse to the sacrifice, and I will show you what you shall do; and you shall anoint for me the one whom I name to you."...*
>
> *Jesse made seven of his sons pass before Samuel, and Samuel said to Jesse, "The LORD has not chosen any of these." Samuel said to Jesse, "Are all your sons here?" And he said, "There remains yet the youngest, but he is keeping the sheep." And Samuel said to Jesse, "Send and bring him;*

for we will not sit down until he comes here." He sent and brought him in. Now he was ruddy, and had beautiful eyes, and was handsome. The LORD *said, "Rise and anoint him; for this is the one." Then Samuel took the horn of oil, and anointed him in the presence of his brothers; and the spirit of the* LORD *came mightily upon David from that day forward.*

1 Samuel 16:1-3, 10-13a

PREPARATION

- Pray for your group participants.
- Make sure every participant has a copy of *Called*. Encourage them to read chapter 2 before the session.
- Read chapter 2, ideally twice—once to get the whole picture, and a second time to note important or memorable passages and topics of discussion.
- Read the Scripture passages included here and, if possible, the rest of the Samuel story. Keep a quality interpretive resource on hand for your or the group's questions.
- Read this session plan and consider what questions and activities will be most useful or important for your particular group, keeping in mind the limits of time available. You may want to write key questions on the markerboard or flip chart ahead of time.
- If any question or topic in the previous sessions was placed in the "parking lot," be sure to find an answer of some kind, or a resource to help the person who raised it.

MATERIALS NEEDED

- Bibles
- markerboard or flip chart
- video (DVD)
- paper and pens for participants to make notes
- nametags (optional)

During the Session

WELCOME AND ICEBREAKER (5-10 MINUTES)

Welcome participants back. Thank them for participating and enriching the group! If you're using nametags, invite participants to fill them out. Ask for volunteers to share how they thought about the last session's topic during the week. Has anyone reflected on their own journeys and experiences of doubt and assurance?

If any questions or topics were placed in the "parking lot" last week, address them here.

After a few minutes of sharing, **read or summarize:** In today's chapter, the author begins by saying this:

> We've all heard that it takes a village to raise a child, but we may not know its sister proverb, "A child belongs not to one parent or home." Both sayings, born out of Africa, mean that it takes a community of people surrounding a child with shared wisdom to influence its proper development. The truth is, many of us have been influenced, not only by our loving, sacrificial parents, but also by mentors or family members who intentionally guided our development in myriad ways.

Ask each participant to share: Tell us about a person, other than a parent, who mentored and guided you in your early life.

After each participant has answered (or passed), thank them.

PRAYER

Lead the group in this or a similar prayer:

Let us pray.

Gracious God, we thank you for the life and witness of your servant Samuel, for the faith of his mother Hannah, and for the guidance of his mentor Eli. We pray that you would enrich your servants here with every good gift. Make us faithful, trustworthy, and brave, that we may bear your creative and saving words to any who need us. We ask this through Christ, our Lord. Amen.

VIDEO (8-10 MINUTES)

Introduce the segment: In today's video, Susan Robb talks about Samuel, who was a priest and prophet of God in ancient Israel. From his longed-for birth to his remarkable career, Samuel's life reflects the many ways God calls God's people, whatever their age or circumstances. Look for connections between the video and the book. We'll discuss them together.

DISCUSSION (20-25 MINUTES)

Read or summarize:

- Today's chapter is about Samuel.
- Samuel lived several hundred years after Abraham and Sarah, after their descendants had escaped from slavery in Egypt and been brought by God into their own land.
- Samuel's mother prayed to God for a son and promised that if God answered her prayer, she would devote that son to God's service. After Samuel is born and weaned from his mother, she gives him to the priest, Eli, at the temple in Shiloh.
- He becomes a priest, a prophet, and a judge of Israel and anoints the first two kings of Israel.
- In this chapter, we encounter Samuel as one who needs guidance, who proves himself trustworthy, and ultimately has to do and say some very hard things.

Ask one or more volunteers to read the story of Hannah and the birth of Samuel in 1 Samuel 1:1-20.

Ask the participants:

- Have you ever poured your soul out to God with the depth and humility of Hannah? How did you feel afterward?
- Has there been a time when you questioned your worth? How did you regain your sense of worth?
- Not knowing if her prayer will be answered, Hannah gets up and is "sad no longer." Why do you think that is?

When God answers Hannah's prayers, she sings a song of praise to God. **Ask a volunteer** to read Hannah's song (1 Samuel 2:1-10) and **another volunteer** to read Mary's song (Luke 1:46-55). **Ask the participants:**

- Do you notice any similarities or echoes? (*Possible answers: rejoicing/ exulting in God; reversal of rich/poor, full/hungry, mighty/lowly*)
- What are some "reversals" that could or should happen in our world or in your life?

After Samuel is weaned, Hannah brings him to the temple. **Ask a volunteer** to read 1 Samuel 1:27-28: " 'For this child I prayed; and the Lord has granted me the petition that I made to him. Therefore, I have lent him to the Lord; as long as he lives, he is given to the Lord.' She left him there for the Lord."

Ask the group:

- How do you think Hannah felt leaving her child at the temple?
- Is there anything in your life that you left or lent to God because it felt to you like a gift?

Say or summarize: In this chapter, the author shares the story of asking God for affirmation from her husband to pursue a seminary education and ordained ministry. "Sometimes, we hear God's voice but need clarity and encouragement from someone else to recognize it." Eli gives Samuel encouragement and instruction for hearing and responding to the word of God.

Read together 1 Samuel 3:1-12. **Ask the participants:**

- Who has been like Eli to you, helping you understand how to hear your calling? Have you done this for someone else?
- The author writes, "Living out our call sometimes requires us to deliver bad news or to engage in the difficult or uncomfortable." When have you had to do this? How did it feel?

Later on, Samuel calls the people to worship only the God of Abraham and not any of the other gods worshipped in the land. He anoints Saul as the first king of Israel, and then he anoints David when Saul falls from God's favor. **Ask:**

- What word(s) do we get from "anointing"? (*chrio, Christ*)
- Do you feel or believe yourself to be "anointed" as a part of the body of Christ? Why or why not?

Finally, Samuel anoints a new king, David, to replace Saul (1 Samuel 16:1-13). Samuel expects one of David's older brothers to be chosen, but instead it is the youngest. **Take a moment to reflect:**

- What was a time you were judged superficially?
- What was a time you judged someone else superficially?

PRAYER ACTIVITY (10–15 MINUTES)

Divide the group into pairs. If there's an odd number, either include yourself or add a third person to a group. Invite the pairs to take turns sharing some concerns that they need help and prayers to address. They may be matters over which they already pray, or they may be things they haven't previously thought to pray over.

In pairs, share an example of each of the following:

- a petition of your heart that you want God to hear and answer;
- something in your life or the world that needs to be "reversed," as in Hannah's and Mary's songs, rather than just made a little better;
- a place in your life where your self-worth needs restoration;
- a mentor for whom you give thanks;
- a place in your life where you need the courage to say or do something difficult.

Ask the participants to take notes for one another's prayers.

CLOSING (5–10 MINUTES)

Say or summarize: The author ends the chapter with the story of young David, son of Jesse, who is identified by God as the one after God's own heart who will become Israel's king. David is the youngest brother, but God does not look on outward appearances. As the author says:

> Abraham is headed into his geriatric years when God calls him to become the faithful father of a multitude of nations. Samuel is a boy when God calls him to begin his prophetic ministry, garnering the trust of his people and providing spiritual and political stability to his nation. David, a young sheepherder, a man after God's own heart, becomes the most successful and one of the longest-reigning kings of Israel (1 Chronicles 14:17; 29:27).

> Whenever you think you can't possibly be of any use to God because you are too old or young, too short or tall, not handsome or pretty or smart or skilled enough, think again.

This week we all have the chance to meditate on those callings we do not think we are prepared or virtuous enough to answer, and on those needs that only God can satisfy for us.

Invite each participant to pray for the five petitions their prayer partner shared with them in the pause provided.

Let us pray.

Gracious God, we give you thanks for your goodness and loving kindness made known to us in the creation and preservation of all that exists. We pray that you would make yourself known to us, your servants, in our every need and our every good act. We pray especially for...

All this we lift up before you, O God, trusting that you hear us, through Jesus Christ our Savior and Lord. Amen.

A Time Such as This

Planning the Session

SESSION GOALS

Participants in this session should have the opportunity to

- learn about the setting, principal characters, and themes of the Book of Esther;
- see the ways in which they have power to influence the world around them;
- listen for the voice of God in competing claims;
- discover whether and how they identify with Queen Esther, Mordecai, or the Persians.

BIBLICAL BACKGROUND

The Book of Esther takes place much later than the stories of Abraham and even Samuel, and many miles from the land of Canaan, where their stories mostly took place. It's a story of the Jewish Diaspora—the portion of the Jewish people deported from the Holy Land after the conquests by the Assyrian and Babylonian empires in the eighth and seventh centuries BC, and who did not return after the Persian empire granted them the right to do so in the sixth century. Esther and her cousin Mordecai are part of this displaced Jewish community, living in the Persian province of Susa even later, in the fifth century. Despite their long separation from the land of Abraham and their assimilation into Persian culture (the name *Mordecai* refers to an ancient Near Eastern deity), they retain a distinct identity and, as the story shows, they could become a target for violence and conspiracy.

> On the seventh day, when the king was merry with wine, he commanded Mehuman, Biztha, Harbona, Bigtha and Abagtha, Zethar and Carkas, the seven eunuchs who attended him, to bring Queen Vashti before the king, wearing the royal crown, in order to show the peoples and the officials her beauty; for she was fair to behold. But Queen Vashti refused to come at the king's command conveyed by the eunuchs. At this the king was enraged, and his anger burned within him....
>
> Then Memucan said in the presence of the king and the officials, "Not only has Queen Vashti done wrong to the king, but also to all the officials and all the peoples who are in all the provinces of King Ahasuerus.... If it pleases the king, let a royal order go out from him, and let it be written among the laws of the Persians and the Medes so that it may not be altered, that Vashti is never again to come before King Ahasuerus; and let the king give her royal position to another who is better than she."
>
> Esther 1:10-12, 16, 19

> Now Esther was admired by all who saw her. When Esther was taken to King Ahasuerus in his royal palace in the tenth month, which is the month of Tebeth, in the seventh year of his reign, the king loved Esther more than all the other women; of all the virgins she won his favor and devotion, so that he set the royal crown on her head and made her queen instead of Vashti.
>
> Esther 2:15b-17

> After these things King Ahasuerus promoted Haman son of Hammedatha the Agagite, and advanced him and set his seat above all the officials who were with him.... When Haman saw that Mordecai did not bow down or do obeisance to him, Haman was infuriated. But he thought it beneath him to lay hands on Mordecai alone. So, having been told who Mordecai's people were, Haman plotted to destroy all

the Jews, the people of Mordecai, throughout the whole kingdom of Ahasuerus.

Esther 3:1, 5-6

When they told Mordecai what Esther had said, Mordecai told them to reply to Esther, "Do not think that in the king's palace you will escape any more than all the other Jews. For if you keep silence at such a time as this, relief and deliverance will rise for the Jews from another quarter, but you and your father's family will perish. Who knows? Perhaps you have come to royal dignity for just such a time as this."

Esther 4:12-14

"Go, gather all the Jews to be found in Susa, and hold a fast on my behalf, and neither eat nor drink for three days, night or day. I and my maids will also fast as you do. After that I will go to the king, though it is against the law; and if I perish, I perish."

Esther 4:16

On the third day Esther put on her royal robes and stood in the inner court of the king's palace, opposite the king's hall. The king was sitting on his royal throne inside the palace opposite the entrance to the palace. As soon as the king saw Queen Esther standing in the court, she won his favor and he held out to her the golden scepter that was in his hand. Then Esther approached and touched the top of the scepter. The king said to her, "What is it, Queen Esther? What is your request? It shall be given you, even to the half of my kingdom."

Esther 5:1-3

So the king and Haman went in to feast with Queen Esther. On the second day, as they were drinking wine, the king again said to Esther, "What is your petition, Queen Esther? It shall be granted you. And what is your request? Even to the half of my kingdom, it shall be fulfilled." Then Queen Esther answered, "If I have won your favor, O king, and if it pleases the king, let my life be given me—that is my petition—and the lives of my people—that is my request. For we have been sold, I and my people, to be destroyed, to be killed, and to be annihilated. If we had been sold merely as slaves, men and women, I would have held my peace; but no enemy can compensate for this damage to the king."

31

Then King Ahasuerus said to Queen Esther, "Who is he, and where is he, who has presumed to do this?"

Esther 7:1-5

Now in the twelfth month, which is the month of Adar, on the thirteenth day, when the king's command and edict were about to be executed, on the very day when the enemies of the Jews hoped to gain power over them, but which had been changed to a day when the Jews would gain power over their foes, the Jews gathered in their cities throughout all the provinces of King Ahasuerus to lay hands on those who had sought their ruin; and no one could withstand them, because the fear of them had fallen upon all peoples. All the officials of the provinces, the satraps and the governors, and the royal officials were supporting the Jews, because the fear of Mordecai had fallen upon them. For Mordecai was powerful in the king's house, and his fame spread throughout all the provinces as the man Mordecai grew more and more powerful.

Esther 9:1-4

PREPARATION

- Pray for your group participants.
- Make sure every participant has a copy of *Called*. Encourage them to read chapter 3 before the session
- Read chapter 3, ideally twice—once to get the whole picture, and a second time to note important or memorable passages and topics of discussion.
- Read the Scripture passages included here and, if possible, the rest of the Book of Esther. Keep a quality interpretive resource on hand for your or the group's questions.
- Read this session plan and consider what questions and activities will be most useful or important for your particular group, keeping in mind the limits of time available. You may want to write key questions on the markerboard or flip chart ahead of time.
- If any question or topic in the previous sessions was placed in the "parking lot," be sure to find an answer of some kind, or a resource to help the person who raised it.

MATERIALS NEEDED

- Bibles
- markerboard or flip chart
- video (DVD)
- paper and pens for participants to make notes
- nametags (optional)

During the Session

WELCOME AND ICEBREAKER (5-10 MINUTES)

Welcome participants back. Thank them for participating and enriching the group! If you're using nametags, invite participants to fill them out. Ask for volunteers to share how they thought about the last session's topic during the week. Has anyone thought about the people who played a formative role for them, or about the hard things their callings required them to say and do?

If any questions or topics were placed in the "parking lot" last week, address them here.

After a few minutes of sharing, **read or summarize:** In today's chapter, the author says, "One person, through one action or one conversation, can change the trajectory of another person's life—or the trajectory of an entire people or nation. Such is the story of Esther." Esther used her charm, her beauty, and her relationship with the ruler of Persia to save her people. Take a moment now to think of a person in your life who could persuade you to do things because of their goodness, their wisdom, or the force of their personality.

After a minute of silence, **ask each participant** to tell the group about that person.

PRAYER

When everyone has shared (or passed), lead the group in this or a similar prayer:

Let us pray.

Gracious God, we give you thanks for the courage and the witness of Esther, the wisdom and boldness of Mordecai, and the perseverance of your people in every age. Grant us grace to see and grasp our own power to influence your world for better, in our own time, grant us courage to use it, and grant us charity and patience for all who are divided from us. We ask this through Jesus Christ our Lord. Amen.

VIDEO (8-10 MINUTES)

Introduce the segment: In this video, Susan Robb will tell us about Esther and the courage she had to seize a moment of influence and save the day for her people. Look for connections between the video and the book. We'll discuss them together.

DISCUSSION (30-35 MINUTES)

Say or summarize:

- Today's chapter is about Esther.
- Her story takes place several centuries after the story of Samuel and in a distant land in the Persian Empire.
- Esther and her cousin Mordecai are Jews dispersed from the Holy Land.
- Esther becomes queen and ends up in a position to thwart a plot to destroy all the Jewish residents of the empire—but not without taking a big personal risk.

Ask a volunteer to read Esther 1:5-20. **Ask the group:**

- Why might Queen Vashti have been unwilling to appear at the king's banquet?
- What attitudes or stereotypes about women are expressed by the king's advisors?

The king starts a search for a new queen. **Ask a volunteer** to read Esther 2:5-11. **Ask the group:**

- What is the relationship between Mordecai and Esther?
- Why does Mordecai tell Esther not to reveal that she is a Jew? Have you ever felt the need to hide part of yourself like that?

ACTIVITY

Say or summarize: Using the paper provided, take two minutes of silence to write down two lists:

- things you have sometimes chosen not to disclose about yourself for whatever reason
- people who have helped you on your way and when (or whether) you've been in touch to thank them

A Time Such as This

This list is just for you—no sharing this time!

After two minutes, **say or summarize:**

- Esther wins over the king and becomes queen.
- Mordecai uncovers a plot against the king and relays it to him through Esther, saving the king's life.
- Still, another man, Haman, is promoted in the king's favor above Mordecai.
- Haman gets angry at Mordecai for not bowing down to him and decides to get revenge by having all the Jews of the empire killed.
- Haman slanders the Jewish people, persuading the king to agree to the killing.

In today's chapter, the author reflects on the hopefulness she experienced watching her children's diverse friendships, and how

> it became apparent that racial tensions had always been simmering under the surface—just as they had been in Persia. There are those still harboring Hatfield-and-McCoy grudges, fears, or beliefs in racial supremacy, as evidenced in Charleston, Charlottesville, and Dallas, and in mosques and churches across the country where we have experienced shootings, bombings, riots, and vandalism.

Ask the participants:

- Jewish law does not forbid bowing down to figures in authority. Why might Mordecai have been unwilling to bow down before Haman?
- The Jewish minority in the Persian empire seems to have coexisted with their neighbors peaceably for many years. What can happen to make people turn against minority groups in this way?

Mordecai sends to Queen Esther to help by appealing to the king. **Ask a volunteer** to read Esther 4:10-17. **Ask the group:**

- Why is Esther reluctant to do what Mordecai asks?
- Do you relate to Esther's dilemma? Are you ever afraid of the consequences of speaking up against an injustice?

ACTIVITY

Say or summarize: Using the paper provided, take two minutes of silence to write down two lists:

- stereotypes and slanders, along with the groups they are applied to
- stereotypes you fear other people might hold about you or people like you

None of these need to be shared.

Say or summarize: Holding a stereotype does not necessarily make you a bad person. We absorb all kinds of stereotypes from an early age. But it's important to know that we hold them, and it's important to know that people are always more complicated than their stereotypes. When we look at the list of stereotypes we think people hold about us, we know this, right? We know that we are not as simple and two-dimensional as those images make us out to be.

Say or summarize: Esther dares to approach the king and is granted an audience. She does not bring up the coming violence against her people (the king still does not know that she's a Jew). Instead she invites the king to a banquet. **Ask a volunteer** to read Esther 7. **Ask the participants:**

- Why did Esther wait until after so much feasting to ask the king to prevent the destruction of her people?
- This is the first time Esther reveals her ethnic identity to the king. Why is that important?

Say or summarize: The king turns against Haman and rescinds the edict that would have exterminated the Jews. Instead he grants the Jews of Persia the right to defend themselves against all their enemies. Esther and Mordecai have saved their people from destruction.

ACTIVITY

Say or summarize: Near the end of this chapter, the author talks about how we overcome differences.

> We are all born for such a time as this. God seeks to use ordinary people, like you and me and a young Jewish girl named Esther, to do extraordinary things and be conduits of God's kingdom on earth. But sometimes we, like Esther, think, "What can I

possibly do? I don't have the skill or the will to make a difference. Someone more qualified should do this. I am so isolated from what is going on 'out there.' Someone else ought to do something about this!"

And

Sitting down over lunch, having conversation, and getting to know one another on a personal level often changes our attitude about people we once thought of as "them."

Esther was placed in a position of influence "for such a time as this," but every time is such a time, and every one of us has *some* kind of influence in our world. We're going to take three more minutes of silence to make three more lists:

- Write down the times your firsthand experience changed your views about a group or an individual.
- Make a list of dangerous injustices or poisonous slanders in our world that need to be repaired.
- Make a list of the ways you can use your influence to repair them.

Think about those stereotypes you wrote down earlier—about others and yourself. Think about when you've been willing to speak out against injustice or bigotry, and when you haven't.

After three minutes, **invite the group** to share parts of their lists.

CLOSING

Say or summarize: Remember that the story ends with a celebration, the festival of Purim. The author writes:

Whenever God provides a means of salvation, historically it is remembered and celebrated. It's important for God's people to remember what God has done on our behalf through the ages, lest we forget we are blessed to be a blessing. God's act of salvation in leading Israel out of slavery in Egypt is celebrated annually at Passover. As Christians, we remember and celebrate our salvation from slavery to sin and death at Christmas and Easter and every time we celebrate Communion. Because the Jews are saved from destruction due to Esther's responding decisively to God's call, Purim is decreed as a festival the Jews are to celebrate annually to remember God's act of salvation.

Keep your lists with you this week to help you remember what God has saved you *from*, and what God has saved you *for*.

Please pray with me:

Almighty God, who holds the days and ages of every kingdom and every life in your almighty hand: Give to us your servants a heart with the boldness and faithfulness of Esther and Mordecai; free us from scorn and slander, both that we give and that we receive. Make us instruments of your peace, justice, and reconciliation in the world. Help us to hear your voice in the midst of the world's disorder, to fold our hands in prayer and in labor, and to heed your calling in our time. Amen.

A Most Reluctant Prophet

Planning the Session

SESSION GOALS

Participants in this session should have the opportunity to

- learn the story of Jonah;
- identify their own experiences of stubbornness and reluctance;
- see the power of God to work everywhere and any time, beyond their specific expectations;
- grasp God's willingness to work despite or through our reluctance.

BIBLICAL BACKGROUND

The Book of Jonah is short and eventful. It's important to take the little time required to read it all yourself before the session. A few key passages are excerpted below.

> Now the word of the LORD came to Jonah son of Amittai, saying, "Go at once to Nineveh, that great city, and cry out against it; for their wickedness has come up before me." But Jonah set out to flee to Tarshish from the presence of the LORD. He went down to Joppa and found a

ship going to Tarshish; so he paid his fare and went on board, to go with them to Tarshish, away from the presence of the LORD....

Then they cried out to the LORD, "Please, O LORD, we pray, do not let us perish on account of this man's life. Do not make us guilty of innocent blood; for you, O LORD, have done as it pleased you." So they picked Jonah up and threw him into the sea; and the sea ceased from its raging. Then the men feared the LORD even more, and they offered a sacrifice to the LORD and made vows.

But the LORD provided a large fish to swallow up Jonah; and Jonah was in the belly of the fish three days and three nights.

Jonah 1:1-3, 14-17

Then Jonah prayed to the LORD his God from the belly of the fish, saying,

> *"I called to the LORD out of my distress,*
>   *and he answered me;*
> *out of the belly of Sheol I cried,*
>   *and you heard my voice.*
> *You cast me into the deep,*
>   *into the heart of the seas,*
>   *and the flood surrounded me;*
> *all your waves and your billows*
>   *passed over me....*
> *The waters closed in over me;*
>   *the deep surrounded me;*
> *weeds were wrapped around my head*
>   *at the roots of the mountains.*
> *I went down to the land*
>   *whose bars closed upon me forever;*
> *yet you brought up my life from the Pit....*

Then the LORD spoke to the fish, and it spewed Jonah out upon the dry land.

Jonah 2:1-3, 5-6, 10

Where can I go from your spirit?
 Or where can I flee from your presence?
If I ascend to heaven, you are there;
 if I make my bed in Sheol, you are there.
If I take the wings of the morning
 and settle at the farthest limits of the sea,
even there your hand shall lead me,
 and your right hand shall hold me fast.
If I say, "Surely the darkness shall cover me,
 and the light around me become night,"
even the darkness is not dark to you;
 the night is as bright as the day,
 for darkness is as light to you.

Psalm 139:7-12

So Jonah set out and went to Nineveh, according to the word of the LORD. Now Nineveh was an exceedingly large city, a three days' walk across. Jonah began to go into the city, going a day's walk. And he cried out, "Forty days more, and Nineveh shall be overthrown!" And the people of Nineveh believed God; they proclaimed a fast, and everyone, great and small, put on sackcloth. . . .

When God saw what they did, how they turned from their evil ways, God changed his mind about the calamity that he had said he would bring upon them; and he did not do it.

Jonah 3:3-5, 10

But this was very displeasing to Jonah, and he became angry. . . . And the LORD said, "Is it right for you to be angry?" Then Jonah went out of the city and sat down east of the city, and made a booth for himself there. He sat under it in the shade, waiting to see what would become of the city.

The LORD God appointed a bush, and made it come up over Jonah, to give shade over his head, to save him from his discomfort; so Jonah was very happy about the bush. But when dawn came up the next day, God appointed a worm that attacked the bush, so that it withered. . . .

But God said to Jonah, "Is it right for you to be angry about the bush?" And he said, "Yes, angry enough to die." Then the LORD said, "You are concerned about the bush, for which you did not labor and which you did not grow; it came into being in a night and perished in a night. And should I not be concerned about Nineveh, that great city, in which there are more than a hundred and twenty thousand persons who do not know their right hand from their left, and also many animals?"

Jonah 4:1, 4-7, 9-11

PREPARATION

- Pray for your group participants.
- Encourage participants to read chapter 4 of *Called* before the session.
- Read chapter 4, ideally twice—once to get the whole picture, and a second time to note important or memorable passages and topics of discussion.
- Read the Book of Jonah. Keep a quality interpretive resource on hand for your or the group's questions.
- Read this session plan and consider what questions and activities will be most useful or important for your particular group, keeping in mind the limits of time available. You may want to write key questions on the markerboard or flip chart ahead of time.
- If any question or topic in the previous sessions was placed in the "parking lot," be sure to find an answer of some kind, or a resource to help the person who raised it.

MATERIALS NEEDED

- Bibles
- Bible atlas, if maps are not included in your copy
- markerboard or flip chart
- video (DVD)
- paper and pens for participants to make notes
- nametags (optional)

During the Session

WELCOME AND ICEBREAKER (5-10 MINUTES)

Welcome participants back. Thank them for participating and enriching the group! If you're using nametags, invite participants to fill them out. Ask for volunteers to share how they thought about the last session's topic during the week. Did anyone think about the influence they have in the world around them? Did anyone speak up or act differently at work or at home after hearing Esther's story?

If any questions or topics were placed in the "parking lot" last week, address them here.

After a minute or two of discussion, **say or summarize:** In today's chapter, the author writes: "When we are certain that God is speaking and calling us to a particular action, most of the time it's easier to follow through on that call because we are sure it is God's will. Other times, we might dig in our heels because of inner conflict." Let's take a minute of silence to think about a time we were afraid or unwilling to go somewhere we had to go.

After a minute has passed, **ask each participant** to share their story. If they don't volunteer it, ask *why* they were unwilling to go somewhere. (*Fear, unfamiliarity, distaste, or discomfort are all likely possibilities.*)

PRAYER

When all have shared (or passed), lead the group in this or a similar prayer: Let us pray.

Gracious God, we give you thanks for Jonah and all your prophets who struggled with reluctance, fear, or unwillingness to answer your calling. We pray that you would soothe and quiet the conflicts within us, that we may more clearly hear your voice and more willingly answer your call; and we pray that we would see you working in our lives and in our world even where we don't yet know to expect you. We ask this through Christ our Lord. Amen.

VIDEO (8-10 MINUTES)

Introduce the segment: In our video today, Susan Robb will tell us more about Jonah and what we can learn from his story—from his reluctance, from God's presence with him, and even from his disappointment and anger. Be mindful of connections between the video and the reading. We'll discuss them together when the video is over.

DISCUSSION (30-40 MINUTES)

Say or summarize: Jonah's story is short and very eventful. His prophetic work takes up all of three verses. The rest of the Book of Jonah concerns his actions immediately before and after that work and the things God does in response to Jonah's actions. But Jonah's particular calling is unusual for a prophet. Instead of speaking to the people of Israel, calling them back to faithful worship and keeping of the Law of God, Jonah is called to bring a prophecy of destruction to Nineveh, the capital city of a hostile empire.

Ask a volunteer to read Jonah 1:1-3. If you have a map available, show the locations of Nineveh, Joppa, and Tarshish (which is all the way in western Spain).

Ask the participants:

- Why did Jonah decide to flee God's calling instead of answering it?
- Have you ever done anything like that?

Jonah is famous for being an unwilling prophet, but he's certainly not the only one. **Ask four participants** (or pairs) to look up the following passages:

- Exodus 4:10-17
- Jeremiah 1:4-9
- Isaiah 6:1-8
- Luke 5:6-10

Ask the participants:

- Why are the prophets and apostles unwilling in these passages? (*Moses doesn't think he can speak well; Jeremiah is too young; Isaiah is a man of unclean lips among people of unclean lips; Peter is a sinful man.*)
- How is Jonah different? (*He doesn't argue with God; he just flees.*)

Ask a volunteer to read the rest of Jonah 1.

Ask the participants:

- What do the sailors do to try to survive the storm? (*call on their gods, cast off the cargo, try to determine who is the target of divine anger*)
- What does Jonah do? (*sleeps in the hold, offers to be thrown overboard*)
- Why doesn't he call on his God? (*He probably fears God's anger against him.*)

Jesus says that the only sign his generation will see is "the sign of the prophet Jonah" (Matthew 12:39-40). **Ask the participants:**

- What does he mean? (*three days in the belly of the fish, as Jesus will lie three days in the tomb*)

- Why is it important that Jonah is rescued by a large fish instead of by, say, an angel?

Ask a volunteer (or two) to read Jonah 2.

Say or summarize: The author writes that "If we compartmentalize our life to contain a 'God box' to keep the Creator in for special occasions while maintaining complete control of the rest of our life, it's disturbing when God crashes in uninvited or acts contrary to our expectations." What does Jonah learn from his time in the belly of the fish? (*that God is present even there, that God is present wherever he might go, that God hears him and preserves him*) Compare with Psalm 139:7-12. Are these words comforting, scary, or both?

Ask a volunteer to read Jonah 3:1-4. **Ask the participants:**

- What message does God give Jonah to proclaim? (*Nineveh will be overthrown in forty days.*)
- Is there any hope in this message? (*No, there is no "unless" or invitation to repent.*)
- Does this help us understand why Jonah was afraid to go to Nineveh?

Ask a volunteer to read the rest of Jonah 3. **Ask the participants:**

- What do the people of Nineveh have in common with the sailors in chapter 1? (*Though they worship other gods, they make prayers and sacrifices to the God of Israel because of Jonah.*)
- What does the king do? (*expand the fast to animals, call for turning from violence*) Why? (*Perhaps God will relent.*)
- What does God do? (*changes God's mind*) Who appears to have spoken more rightly about God—Jonah or the king at Nineveh?

Say or summarize: Something strange happens when this immoral city encounters the unwilling prophet—they believe him! And they act to avert a disaster! Take a moment to think of a time God has used you despite your reluctance and something unexpected happened. Write it down in your notes. Invite participants to share if they wish.

Ask a volunteer to read Jonah 4:1-5. **Say or summarize:** The author says in this section,

> Over and over again, the Lord forgives the people of Israel for turning away, for worshipping other gods, and for oppressing

the orphan, widow, and alien. The Lord does the same for Jonah. We are always okay when God forgives us for hurting others or turning our backs on God, but we have a much more difficult time with God offering forgiveness to "them."

Jonah, like all his people, has a legitimate complaint against the power and cruelty of Nineveh. **Ask the participants:**

- Are there people or places you have been, or would be, unwilling to forgive or see God forgive? Think beyond individuals to whole citizens or nations (like Nineveh).

Ask a volunteer to read the rest of Jonah 4. **Ask the participants:**

- Why do you think God gives Jonah the bush and then takes it away?
- Why does God mention the animals?

Two times God asks Jonah, "Is it right for you to be angry?" Let's take two minutes to think about the last few times we've been angry with someone. Write them down. Then ask yourself God's question—"Is it right for you to be angry?" Maybe the answer is yes, maybe the answer is no. The important thing is to ask!

CLOSING

Say or summarize: The story of Jonah ends without being resolved. Is Jonah still angry? Does Jonah understand his purpose better? Let's take a minute to write down (or imagine) what Jonah might say, later, to someone who thinks he or she might be called to be a prophet. How might Jonah feel looking back on this experience? How might his faith in God, or his understanding of God, have changed? What would he tell that person to do if he or she were to experience a calling from God?

Let us pray.

Patient and merciful God, we thank you for the second chances you grant to your servants, and we thank you for the power of your Word spoken by even the reluctant and unwilling. Help us to trust your love and mercy and share with any we encounter—even our enemies and those who wish us harm. Amen.

I Have Seen the Lord!

Planning the Session

SESSION GOALS

Participants in this session should have the opportunity to

- learn the story of Mary Magdalene;
- describe the importance of community to their experience of faith;
- discover how Jesus is present in "means of grace" even when we struggle to see him;
- understand their calling as distinct from their status or their credentials.

BIBLICAL BACKGROUND

Soon afterwards he went on through cities and villages, proclaiming and bringing the good news of the kingdom of God. The twelve were with him, as well as some women who had been cured of evil spirits and infirmities: Mary, called Magdalene, from whom seven demons had gone out, and Joanna, the wife of Herod's steward Chuza, and Susanna, and many others, who provided for them out of their resources.

Luke 8:1-3

Many women were also there [at the site of Jesus' crucifixion], looking on from a distance; they had followed Jesus from Galilee and had provided for him. Among them were Mary Magdalene, and Mary the mother of James and Joseph, and the mother of the sons of Zebedee.

Matthew 27:55-56

When the sabbath was over, Mary Magdalene, and Mary the mother of James, and Salome bought spices, so that they might go and anoint him. And very early on the first day of the week, when the sun had risen, they went to the tomb.

Mark 16:1-2

Early on the first day of the week, while it was still dark, Mary Magdalene came to the tomb and saw that the stone had been removed from the tomb. So she ran and went to Simon Peter and the other disciple, the one whom Jesus loved, and said to them, "They have taken the Lord out of the tomb, and we do not know where they have laid him." . . .

But Mary stood weeping outside the tomb. As she wept, she bent over to look into the tomb; and she saw two angels in white, sitting where the body of Jesus had been lying, one at the head and the other at the feet. They said to her, "Woman, why are you weeping?" She said to them, "They have taken away my Lord, and I do not know where they have laid him." When she had said this, she turned around and saw Jesus standing there, but she did not know that it was Jesus. Jesus said to her, "Woman, why are you weeping? Whom are you looking for?" Supposing him to be the gardener, she said to him, "Sir, if you have carried him away, tell me where you have laid him, and I will take him away." Jesus said to her, "Mary!" She turned and said to him in Hebrew, "Rabbouni!" (which means Teacher). Jesus said to her, "Do not hold on to me, because I have not yet ascended to the Father. But go to my brothers and say to them, 'I am ascending to my Father and your Father, to my God and your God.'" Mary Magdalene went and announced to the disciples, "I have seen the Lord"; and she told them that he had said these things to her.

John 20:1-2, 11-18

PREPARATION

- Pray for your group participants.
- Encourage participants to read chapter 5 of *Called* before the session.
- Read chapter 5, ideally twice—once to get the whole picture, and a second time to note important or memorable passages and topics of discussion.
- Read the passages above and all of John 20. Keep a quality interpretive resource on hand for your or the group's questions.
- Read this session plan and consider what questions and activities will be most useful or important for your particular group, keeping in mind the limits of time available. You may want to write key questions on the markerboard or flip chart ahead of time.
- If any question or topic in the previous sessions was placed in the "parking lot," be sure to find an answer of some kind, or a resource to help the person who raised it.

MATERIALS NEEDED

- Bibles
- markerboard or flip chart
- video (DVD)
- paper and pens for participants to make notes
- nametags (optional)

During the Session

WELCOME AND ICEBREAKER (5-10 MINUTES)

Welcome participants back. Thank them for participating and enriching the group! If you're using nametags, invite participants to fill them out. Ask for volunteers to share how they thought about the last session's topic during the week. Did anyone think about anger differently? Did anyone face reluctance and overcome it?

If any questions or topics were placed in the "parking lot" last week, address them here.

Say or summarize: In today's chapter, the author writes:

In most of these stories, those who are called worry that they aren't good enough for the task to which they are summoned, or others don't think they're good enough, or worthy enough. They are too old, too young, too reluctant, too inexperienced—or too female. However, they are assured of God's presence that prepares, empowers, and encourages them at each step. They are worthy of the call placed upon them precisely because of the One who calls.

Let's take a minute of silence and think of a time you were faced with a task or a role you did not think you were qualified or good enough for.

After a minute has passed, **ask each participant** to share. What was the task or role? Why did they worry about their qualifications? What happened?

PRAYER

After each participant has shared or passed, pray this or a similar prayer:
Let us pray.

Faithful and abiding God, we give you thanks that your blessed Son restored Mary Magdalene to wholeness of body and spirit and made her the first to proclaim his resurrection. By her witness and faithfulness, help us to see him who calls us to proclaim your kingdom and know his presence, who lives and reigns with you and the Holy Spirit, one God, now and forever. Amen.

VIDEO (8-10 MINUTES)

Introduce the segment: In this video, Susan Robb will tell us about Mary Magdalene. She's a disciple with a complicated (and probably unfair!) reputation, she has an important role in the community of disciples, and she is the first messenger (or "apostle") of Jesus' resurrection. Look for connections between the video and the chapter. We'll discuss them together after the video is over.

DISCUSSION

Say or summarize:

- After four chapters about Old Testament figures, today we're hearing about a disciple of Jesus in the New Testament.
- While historically a lot of attention has focused on the twelve men in Jesus' inner circle, it's clear from the Gospel accounts that women played a large and essential role in the community.

- Mary Magdalene is especially notable among these women.

Ask the participants:

- What is your image of Mary Magdalene? When you hear or see her name, what comes to mind?

Ask a volunteer to read Luke 8:1-3. **Ask the participants:**

- The Gospel of Luke says that seven demons were cast out of Mary Magdalene. What are some demons you've encountered in your life or in people close to you?
- The author writes: "Jesus has used and continues to use various people in my own life to help drive out demons and bring healing. . . . Jesus uses my husband daily (as well as mentors and friends) to help drive demons from my life." Have you ever experienced healing like this?
- How did it feel?

The author writes:

> Mary is labeled, five centuries after her stories are recorded in the Bible, as demon-possessed, a sinner, and, because in later centuries women's "sin" was associated with sexuality, she becomes a whore and prostitute. Talk about her reputation preceding her! Mary has historically gotten a bad rap. Some still perpetuate this bad reputation, even though scripturally Mary Magdalene is never portrayed as a prostitute or as being guilty of any sexual sin. However, Jesus always treats her with love and dignity, and she reciprocates. In turn, Jesus gives her one of the greatest gifts, the responsibility and privilege of being the first to proclaim the gospel message.

Ask the participants:

- Have you ever been labeled or misjudged in an unflattering or harmful way?
- How did you feel about it?
- Did you (or anyone else) do anything to correct the label?
- Can you think of anyone else whose reputation needs to be corrected or restored to them?

Say or summarize: Mary and the other women supported Jesus and his disciples with their resources. The author writes:

> Mary and her sisters in faith band together. Together they follow. Together they learn, listen, discuss, and support. They are there not only for Jesus, but for one another. One of them alone cannot provide for Jesus and all of the needs of his disciples. But together they can. They can do more for one another, as well. When they pool their resources and come together, they are stronger than they are alone.

Ask the participants:

- How has your faith community supported you?
- How have you supported your faith community?
- Is God perhaps calling you to support your faith community in a new way?

Say or summarize: The author writes: "We find in Mary Magdalene a person who has staying power." While most of the male disciples flee the scene of Jesus' crucifixion, Mary and the other women remain.

Ask a volunteer to read Matthew 27:50-55 and Mark 16:1-2. **Ask the participants:**

- Why was it important for the Gospel writers to record the people who stayed with Jesus?
- Why do you think some people fled? Why do you think some stayed?
- Has there ever been a situation where you had to "stay" or "flee," perhaps when someone close to you was suffering? Why did you choose the way you did?

Say or summarize: Later in this chapter, the author tells the story of the death of her cousin, with whom she was very close, and the "dark night of the soul" that followed. Experiencing this sense of loss, she describes looking for Jesus in the many "means of grace" that church presents. And when her grief didn't abate, she goes to a Habitat for Humanity site to work. **Ask the participants:**

- What are the "means of grace" that assure you of Christ's presence?
- Have you ever needed more than those means of grace? If so, where did you find it?

Ask a volunteer to read John 20:1-3. **Ask the participants:**

- Why is it important that Mary is the first to the tomb?
- What does she think has happened?

Ask a volunteer to read John 20:4-18. **Ask the participants:**

- What did "the other disciple" believe?
- Where does he, with Peter, go? Why?
- What does Mary Magdalene do? Why?

At first, Mary can't recognize Jesus. As the author says, "Haven't we all experienced a time in our lives when we were so consumed by grief, fear, or panic that it was difficult to see Jesus in our midst?" **Ask the participants:**

- What was a time in your life when you couldn't recognize Jesus?
- What does Jesus do to make Mary recognize him? (*calls her by her name*)
- What does Jesus tell her to do?
- The author notes that Mary delivers "the first sermon of the Christian faith." What is it?

The author writes: "We can't cling to our own narrow view of Jesus if we are to become all that he desires, nor can we stay holding on to Jesus in our comfortable church pews and auditorium seats." She tells the story of a priest who brought the processional cross out of the sanctuary and into a march with Martin Luther King Jr. **Ask the participants:**

- How does your community bring the Resurrection into the world around it?
- Where else does the proclamation of the risen Christ need to be heard in your world?
- What is your role in making that happen?

CLOSING

Say or summarize: Unlike the other stories we've looked at before, Mary Magdalene's story is not one of overcoming doubt, missteps, or reluctance. Her story is brief, but it is one of tenacious faith.

The Scriptures don't have more to say about Mary's life after the day of Jesus' resurrection. But maybe we can guess. Let's take a couple of minutes to imagine what Mary might have said to a younger Christian who was wrestling with his or her calling and thought that he or she was not qualified for the task or not important enough to do it. **Ask the participants:**

- What lessons would she draw from her own experience?
- What could she say about the Jesus that Christians worship? Use your paper to take notes if you wish.

After two minutes have passed, **invite participants** to share their answers. When everyone who wishes to has shared, close with this or a similar prayer:

Lord God, we thank you for calling us through your Word, for healing us through your compassion, and for giving us grace to participate in your own generosity. As you called, strengthened, blessed, and sent Mary Magdalene, so we ask that you call, strengthen, bless, and send us to those places that wait for the dawn of resurrection. We ask this through Jesus your Son, our Healer and Savior. Amen.

Leaning In

Planning the Session

SESSION GOALS

Participants in this session should have the opportunity to

- identify with the role and position of the "Beloved Disciple";
- think about what it means to "bear fruit";
- discern their own vocations as disciples.

BIBLICAL BACKGROUND

In the beginning was the Word, and the Word was with God, and the Word was God. He was in the beginning with God. All things came into being through him, and without him not one thing came into being. What has come into being in him was life, and the life was the light of all people. The light shines in the darkness, and the darkness did not overcome it....

He was in the world, and the world came into being through him; yet the world did not know him. He came to what was his own, and his own people did not accept him. But to all who received him, who believed in his name, he gave power to become children of God, who were born, not of blood or of the will of the flesh or of the will of man, but of God.

And the Word became flesh and lived among us, and we have seen his glory, the glory as of a father's only son, full of grace and truth. (John testified to him and cried out, "This was he of whom I said, 'He who comes after me ranks ahead of me because he was before me.'") From his fullness we have all received, grace upon grace. The law indeed was given through Moses; grace and truth came through Jesus Christ. No one has ever seen God. It is God the only Son, who is close to the Father's heart, who has made him known.

John 1:1-5, 10-18

After he had washed their feet, had put on his robe, and had returned to the table, he said to them, "Do you know what I have done to you? You call me Teacher and Lord—and you are right, for that is what I am. So if I, your Lord and Teacher, have washed your feet, you also ought to wash one another's feet. For I have set you an example, that you also should do as I have done to you."

John 13:12-15

"I am the true vine, and my Father is the vinegrower. He removes every branch in me that bears no fruit. Every branch that bears fruit he prunes to make it bear more fruit. You have already been cleansed by the word that I have spoken to you. Abide in me as I abide in you. Just as the branch cannot bear fruit by itself unless it abides in the vine, neither can you unless you abide in me. I am the vine, you are the branches. Those who abide in me and I in them bear much fruit, because apart from me you can do nothing. Whoever does not abide in me is thrown away like a branch and withers; such branches are gathered, thrown into the fire, and burned. If you abide in me, and my words abide in you, ask for whatever you wish, and it will be done for you. My Father is glorified by this, that you bear much fruit and become my disciples. As the Father has loved me, so I have loved you; abide in my love. If you keep my commandments, you will abide in my love, just as I have kept my Father's commandments and abide in his love. I have said these things to you so that my joy may be in you, and that your joy may be complete.

'This is my commandment, that you love one another as I have loved you. No one has greater love than this, to lay down one's life for one's friends. You are my friends if you do what I command you. I do not call you servants any longer, because the servant does not know what the master is doing; but I have called you friends, because I have made known to you everything that I have heard from my Father. You did not choose me but I chose you. And I appointed you to go and bear fruit, fruit that will last, so that the Father will give you whatever you ask him in my name. I am giving you these commands so that you may love one another.'

John 15:1-17

"Little children, I am with you only a little longer. You will look for me; and as I said to the Jews so now I say to you, 'Where I am going, you cannot come.' I give you a new commandment, that you love one another. Just as I have loved you, you also should love one another. By this everyone will know that you are my disciples, if you have love for one another."

John 13:33-35

Meanwhile, standing near the cross of Jesus were his mother, and his mother's sister, Mary the wife of Clopas, and Mary Magdalene. When Jesus saw his mother and the disciple whom he loved standing beside her, he said to his mother, "Woman, here is your son." Then he said to the disciple, "Here is your mother." And from that hour the disciple took her into his own home.

John 19:25b-27

PREPARATION

- Pray for your group participants.
- Encourage participants to read chapter 6 of *Called* before the session.
- Read chapter 6, ideally twice—once to get the whole picture, and a second time to note important or memorable passages and topics of discussion.
- Read the passages above. Keep a quality interpretive resource on hand for your or the group's questions.
- Read this session plan and consider what questions and activities will be most useful or important for your particular group, keeping in mind the limits of time available. You may want to write key questions on the markerboard or flip chart ahead of time.

- If any question or topic in the previous sessions was placed in the "parking lot," be sure to find an answer of some kind, or a resource to help the person who raised it.

MATERIALS NEEDED

- Bibles
- markerboard or flip chart
- video (DVD)
- paper and pens for participants to make notes
- nametags (optional)

During the Session

WELCOME AND ICEBREAKER (5-10 MINUTES)

Welcome participants back. Thank them for participating and enriching the group! If you're using nametags, invite participants to fill them out. Ask for volunteers to share how they thought about the last session's topic during the week. Did anyone think about how and where they might proclaim the resurrection of Jesus? or about having to overcome the feeling of being unqualified?

If any questions or topics were placed in the "parking lot" last week, address them here.

Say or summarize: In this chapter, the author writes:

> "Follow me." It's an imperative Jesus uses twenty-two times in the Gospels. Following can be costly. It may require leaving a livelihood or a family business, as most of these fishermen experienced.... It may involve ridicule and opposition.... It may be dangerous.... However, our only job as disciples is to follow.

Let's take a minute of silence and think of a person we have "followed"—someone we found compelling, who challenged us, and who called out the best in us.

After a minute has passed, **ask each participant** to share.

PRAYER

When everyone has shared, lead the group in this or a similar prayer:

Let us pray.

O God, Lord of the prophets and apostles, patriarchs and matriarchs: open our hearts to the example of those who followed your Son. May we, like they, feel his kind and cleansing touch, share his mind, and go forth to make disciples wherever we go. We ask this through Jesus, our Savior and our friend. Amen.

VIDEO (8-10 MINUTES)

Introduce the segment: In this video, Susan Robb will tell us about the intimacy of the Beloved Disciple with Jesus, and how that intimacy can be mirrored in our own lives as disciples of Jesus. As you watch, look for connections between the work of the disciples and your own gifts, and between the book and the video. We'll discuss them together.

DISCUSSION

Say or summarize:

- Today, in our last session, we're not really talking about one individual's story. Instead we're talking about the figure of the "Beloved Disciple."
- The Beloved Disciple, or "the disciple whom Jesus loved," is mentioned only in the Gospel of John, appearing in chapter 13 and recurring until the end.
- The author writes:

  Many think the Beloved Disciple is actually John, who was part of Jesus' inner circle of friends along with Peter and James, and to whom authorship of this Gospel is attributed. Others believe that the Beloved Disciple is Lazarus, whose death Jesus wept over, and whom Jesus raised from the dead. Still others propose Jesus' brother James, or even Mary Magdalene, as the "one whom Jesus loved." While there are good reasons to name each as the Beloved Disciple, none can be proven.

- **Ask the participants:** Why is it significant that this disciple is not named? (*many reasons, but important one is that we can identify with him or her*)

Ask one volunteer to read John 1:1, 14, 18 and **another volunteer** to read John 13:23. **Say or summarize:** As the author says, the word expressing the Word's relationship with God is the same as the word used to express the Beloved Disciple's position leaning into Jesus. **Ask the participants:**

- What do these verses tell you about Jesus' relationship with God?
- What do they tell you about the relationship between Jesus and "the one whom Jesus loved"?
- What would it look like for you to lean against Jesus' breast? Have you ever felt that kind of intimacy with Jesus?
- How can you better "lean into" Jesus?

ACTIVITY

Say or summarize: In this chapter, the author tells a story about some women who were moved to help someone get out of exploitative work and who founded a ministry dedicated to helping people who have been trafficked. On your note paper, make two columns. In the left-hand column, write down the things that hold you back from doing something like that. It can be work, money, anxiety, other obligations, a sense of fear or discomfort—anything at all. Then in the right-hand column, write down the things you would do if all those factors went away. What need would you devote yourself to meeting? Where and how would you live out your calling?

After two minutes of silence, **invite participants** to share their answers if they wish.

After everyone who wishes to has shared, **say or summarize:** The theme of "abiding" in the love of Jesus is important in the Gospel According to John. Jesus compares his disciples to branches abiding or remaining with Jesus, the vine.

Invite a volunteer to read John 15:1-11. **Ask the participants:**

- How do you "abide" in Jesus in your own life as a Christian?
- The author says: "In my life, it is evident when I am abiding." Can you tell when you are "abiding" in Jesus' love, and when you're not?

After everyone who wishes to has shared, **say or summarize:**

- In John's Gospel, mutual love among the disciples is the most important marker of their identity.
- As Jesus says in John 13:35: "By this everyone will know that you are my disciples, if you have love for one another."
- The author writes:

Our obedience to Christ's call to love one another is a transformational witness to those around us and to the rest of the world. When we love each other well, our actions provide a testimony to others of what it looks like to be a Christian. When we love each other well, we bless others and draw them closer to the One who wants to abide in them. Our loving actions invite them to become part of the family of God.

* Family is an important image in the Gospels and in Christian life generally.

Ask a volunteer to read John 19:25b-27. **Say or summarize:** The author says, "Jesus' mother and the Beloved Disciple are not flesh-and-blood relatives, but they have developed a kinship, a spiritual genealogy, through their oneness in Jesus and the Father. There is an intentionality to creating Christian community."
Ask the participants:

* When have you experienced this "oneness" with someone through your faith?
* What does it feel like?
* What do you want people who are not part of your faith community to see, or to imagine, when they see you living out your faith?

CLOSING

Say or summarize: The author writes: "When I look out over the congregation on a Sunday morning, I know that many of them come to worship with one question in mind: Is this true? Is it true that God lives and gives us life?"

People experience faith in different ways. Some people need to have a lot of questions answered before they can make the movement of faith. Some people do not. The Beloved Disciple did not have a full picture of who Jesus was, or of what he himself had seen. But then neither did Abraham, Samuel, Esther, Jonah, or Mary Magdalene. The life of discipleship is like the old saying: "I don't know what the future holds, but I know who holds the future."

As the author says,

> our only job as disciples is to follow: Follow where we are led and stay near the shepherd. Follow his voice. Follow the example of our Lord as he stays near the breast of the Father. Follow and emulate the Beloved Disciple leaning on the breast of Jesus.

Follow the example of the Beloved Disciple in caring for our brothers and sisters in Christ, our family.

Ask the participants: As we conclude today, I ask you to consider, and make notes if you wish:

- Where do you hear the voice of Jesus leading you?
- How can you stay near to Jesus?
- How are you being called to care for your brothers and sisters in Christ?

After two or three minutes of silence (or more if needed), **invite the participants** to share if they wish. Thank them for participating!

You may close with prayer or with this litany that follows:

Litany

Leader:
We give you thanks almighty God for your servants of every time and every place.
People:
We praise and thank you, O God.

For the power of your calling in every age
We praise and thank you, O God.

For Abraham and Sarah
We praise and thank you, O God.

For Samuel and all the prophets
We praise and thank you, O God.

For Esther and all who fight oppression
We praise and thank you, O God.

For Jonah and all who take risks
We praise and thank you, O God.

For Mary Magdalene and all who held vigil at the cross and tomb
We praise and thank you, O God.

For James, John, and all the apostles, for all who helped and followed them,
for all who left home and family for the sake of the gospel
We praise and thank you, O God.

For those who have answered your call in every time and place
We praise and thank you, O God.

For our own callings, that you would make them clear and strengthen our steps
We praise and thank you, O God.

Let us pray:

Gracious God, we thank you for all those callings we have heard and have yet to hear. Grant us open eyes and ears for all that you would have us do. Make us the means of your peace and reconciliation. Teach us to pray more faithfully and boldly. And remember your servants in our times of trial. All this we ask through Jesus Christ, our Savior and Lord. Amen.

CPSIA information can be obtained
at www.ICGtesting.com
Printed in the USA
LVHW030043050619
620147LV00004B/4